Vol. 1 Issue 1

© Copyright Agony's Point Press
agonyspoint.substack.com

ISBN: 9798872166290

All rights reserved. No part of this work may be copied or reproduced in any way without the express written permission of the author(s) and the publisher.

Drums of Tophet

In a few brief months since the conception of this Journal and in the immediate weeks surrounding the release of our flagship title, *Sword of Undeath*, all realize without any possibility of doubt that the planet upon which we reside is entering into a new phase of a new and horrifying era regardless of whatever religion or ideological belief system to which one may or may not prescribe. With mass death and quite literal world-war style ground combat taking place in Ukraine and other conflicts across the globe the most arresting flashpoint to many has been the recent outbreak of war between Israel and Gaza with now more than ten-thousand reported casualties in a matter of weeks at date of writing and with many thousands more likely by the time this issue goes to print.

According to multiple comparative scriptures of antiquity we are now well underway into what is alternately referred to as the Kali-yuga, the Iron Age, Wolf Age, etc. Whatever details may differ according to respective traditions all such scriptures agree that we live beneath the foreshadowing of a final and apocalyptic battle to come - the war of all wars - end-times prophecy here and now before our very eyes.

In the epic *Völuspá* a seer describes the qualities of Ragnarok to Wodan:

It sates itself on the life-blood of fated men,
paints red the powers' homes with crimson gore.
Black become the sun's beams in the summers that follow,
weathers all treacherous.
Do you still seek to know? And what?

Present in *Sri Kalki Purana* and numerous Vedic literature, scenes of nearly incomprehensible slaughter and rapid deterioration of mankind and overall environment second by second.

A withering and horrible landscape ruled over by insane despots where the populace is reduced to living underground hiding from a sun grown large and malevolent which scorches the earth, the people resorting to cannibalism and subsisting on human flesh until the ongoing degradation ultimately culminates in a merciless and genocidal bloodbath.

Drums of Tophet

In Biblical tradition mirrored in Judaic and Islamic texts with origin point in much older texts of the Assyrians, the rise of Gog and Magog when the Antichrist will rise in the prelude to Armageddon.

It is the purpose of Agony's Point Press and this publication to present to select readership topics salient to these times.

While temporal human ideologies of whatever stripe seek to either constrain the incessant waves of horror that threaten to engulf or manipulate the currents toward some curated end-game conceived by speculative contrivance it is our position that the writ has already been written - all that we now observe and see is symptomatic not of mortal error but rather the work of hideous entities possessed of indescribable psychic fury.

Ours is the black speech, the hideous incantations that - joining together in infernal and fell chorus - invoke confrontation with the undead in all their horror.

In the Valley of Hinnom, the ancient residing place of the Rephaite, the drums of Tophet were beaten to drown out the sounds of screaming from the children being sacrificed to Moloch. As the funerary smoke of a world aflame chokes the globe those drums beat once again. Walk with us through the fire.

Agony's Point
November 9, 2023

Ghastly Spectres Coming Forth By Night

Conceptual distortion is a mechanism often utilized in LHP praxis as well as in religion in general whatever its touted morality or lack thereof. Engaging in arcana - the worship of demons and demigods, divinities and devils in the form of idols or icons (shorthandedly referred to as "deity worship" in some New Religious Movements) can be classified thusly. As one looks and meditates on the face, limbs and posture of an idol while making offerings before it, waving a lamp of fire, anointing with water and unguents day after day, year after year, one begins mirroring the deity. Similarly to the example of if one looked into a mirror and instead of vision of the physical body saw something altogether alien reflecting back, as one stares upon the face of the deity in the context of worship one's own self-concept begins to conform to that which is the object of worship and veneration. No longer separated as the supplicant so venerating and the target of veneration one reaches a state of unity.

Not her alone but yourself who stands fanged with red tongue protruding, the khadag of sacrifice raised aloft in a sky where vultures circle above in carrion thirst for the dead which litter the ground beneath - not her but you whose neck the hue of midnight is encircled with a garland of skulls, you who ride upon the corpse vahana through time and space from before the world was conceived to the destructive flames of universal dissolution that will destroy all at the end of days. No longer simply "self-concept as an accomplice of evil" but rather the source of all evil itself.

Amidst secular contemporary society there is at present a great amount of hand-wringing over the quantum increases in technology and AI specifically. In tandem with the elation of technological revolution lies the dread omens which accompany revolutions of any sort as the finite mind of man looks into the future abyss encapsulating an infinity of possible outcomes.

Only a few short decades ago there was still much cautionary polemic concerning innovations we now take for granted such as television, often coming from traditional circles who (rightly so) realized the potential for such technology to bring about a separation from "concrete reality" and its consequential utilization in implanting insidious mind viruses that could ultimately poison the waters of a hitherto tranquil and homogeneous collective existence.

Violence and transgression, the enticing and sometimes obscene choreography of eros and the equally alluring and potentially catastrophic tandava dance of pain and lethality are the two infernal horns which, thrust up from the earth into the firmament, cause even the denizens of the heavens to weep. Curated, brief and censored glimpses into an arena of bombs and bloodshed, horror and death during American operations in Vietnam and Cambodia destabilized the minds and from there the social equilibrium of those on the homefront, though separated by thousands of miles from the action. Secrets hitherto clandestine and only carried in the memories of those who had seen combat personally were now revealed to all and thrust upon the social consciousness of a people unable to process the grisly brutality that such vistas afford. With the granite foundation of society beginning to soften and opportunities for havoc now presented the enemies of the state entered in - foreign actors who via hook or crook would erode old social orders and create a dissonance that still reverberates to this day through the infiltration of beliefs, concepts and ideologies that are specifically designed to harm.

Fast forward several decades further and as the dust from the WTC attacks had yet to settle the beginning of the war on terror with all that would and still entails. "Terror met by greater terror" but most importantly the term alone injected, emphasized and hammered into the citizenry again and again and again like some hideous mantra: *terror* as the axis upon which spins the universe, *terror* the designator which describes a thing, a place, a person - a concept, an aesthetic. All that is threat and bringing upon it like the four horsemen of the Apocalypse or the horrible smoke of universal material destruction - threat compounded upon threat.

A person visits a newsstand on the streets of a major metropolitan city or at the soda counter in rural America and sees images on the glossy special report magazines churned out in vast quantities with regular superseding editions - men in orange jumpsuits, faces obscured by black capture hoods, goggles and shackled with gleaming steel restraints. These the enemy, trussed up for their own safety but also for our own security. Thus with a slight diversion in import mechanisms once relegated to the black world were let loose in stark visual relief into the collective consciousness. "The gloves are off" - the ghastly spectres of intelligence "coming forth by night" into every town and village.

Once so immediate and so pressing in the public consciousness, these events are now decades past – many who experienced them now gone and many reading these words today not yet alive to see them. The revelations of television and print journalism who "brought the war home" in a fashion once unprecedented has brought us to now – a time where most individuals in the developed world technically exist as cyborgs due to afforded technological advancement. In this, levels for extreme distortion of self-concept exist and are bearing fruit – from popular focus on transhumanism, alternate sexuality, identity shifts and more. Images of violence are easily had as butchery and mayhem are broadcast from the ground to anyone who cares to look and, like bloodthirsty dakinis serviceable to the black goddess of destruction, politicians and pundits gleefully embrace the commodification of civilian casualties and child death with full force.

Staring into the abyss allows all the entities within that hideous backwards darkness to stare back and through contagion and spiritual reciprocation one ultimately begins to be changed even if the effort leveraged is slight or approached with the determination of a seasoned fanatic.

For adepts of the black arts, for the intergenerational Satanists who possess within themselves the blood of that old dragon "thrown to earth" now reincarnate in the DNA and RNA strands of that most secret and hidden strata walking upon the earth and also for those who follow that other sideward and unclean path inviting possession by the undead – hostile intelligences from an age gone by – such brutal change is understood. Yet so let it be emphasized and emphasized beyond any shadow of a doubt that the distortion of self-concept which you understand on a singular level or within the close confines of clandestine cells amongst fellow-travelers of the night breed is now occurring on a worldwide scope and though the destination may be different certain of the mechanisms utilized - the same.

Dark mothers horrifying in their countenance, cruel and wicked in their intent once accessed only by black pilgrimage to hidden shrines in remote wilderness or through secret interdimensional portals through methods most occult now cast their withering gaze upon all humanity from vantage points in hideous Astral Sky – all shall be disciplined, all subject to their horrifying will. None shall deny them. Dark forces ungovernable cannot be governed. No spell will keep them out. "Every knee shall bow, every tongue confess" in the series of events leading irrevocably toward the Final Harvest.

Howls from East: Interview with Commander Butcher of MKY

CAVEAT LECTOR: Underground publications shouldn't as a rule find it necessary to issue preambles to content and, ideally, there shouldn't be.

In this case however and as a small press operating without the corporate backing enjoyed by the mainstream publishing industry the editors of *Drums of Tophet* consider it prudent to do so.

MKY has been mentioned in media reports worldwide and covered in various governmental briefings. There has been speculation emanating from both as to whether or not they exist as Satan incarnate, a highly dangerous organic, terrorist criminal threat, an intelligence-driven provocation to fracture society from within in Russia or – according to some – literally "non-existent."

Whatever the case may be the name, fame and alleged pastimes of MKY have been pushed into the public sphere and yet everything about them remains for the most part cloaked in mystery.

To date and to our knowledge there has only been one direct interview with MKY in English. By what we can infer from cursory knowledge that interview was intended as an express promotion of MKY as political fellow-travelers which is certainly within their rights.

If NBC interviews Al-Qaeda no one bats an eye as to intention (though perhaps they should) whereas if Al-Qaeda interviews Al-Qaeda it's incitement and the publication itself becomes illegal (in some parts of the world at least.) Should a gothic zine interview a serial killer its considered harmless if not distasteful - if a communist party newsletter in the West interviews a South American partisan group that is proscribed as a prohibited organization in the country where the publication is issued it's usually ignored. The fulcrum in all the examples above center around the reputation of the organ so publishing and the perception , speculatively based, as to the intention of such an organ. In the United States freedom of press is a constitutionally guaranteed right yet there are many who foment against it. As a publication having just been launched *Drums of Tophet* has yet to establish a reputation within such a schema.

Agony's Point Press is the Horrifying Voice of Wamphyrism, premiere Satanic theory and predatory spirituality. As such as its primary Journal we would be remiss in not leading you upon razor's edge to the heart of darkness regarding Satanism in the world today. Where others offer only rumor from afar, we take you to the source. We introduce to you Commander Butcher, MKY.

APP: Although everyone knows about Ukraine and Russia conflict, knowledge of MKU is still mystery to many outside the region. Can you explain to our readership some about the foundation of MKU and the circumstances which led it to come to worldwide attention after the arrests in Russia?

MKU: We National-Socialists have our war against all governments, their system isn't in our interest.

Personally I support Azov Battalion and Misanthropic Division on Ukrainian side, also most on Russian side in war are junkies so it's genocide of our people.

MKU/MMC (Maniacs Murder Cult) was created by Yegor Krasnov who had very dark and hard childhood, from his sayings most of his family members were mentally ill. He started to make snuff movies on his video camera, he did manhunt style videos and was inspired by NS/WP like organizations. It grew very fast and by 2019 group became very popular amongst Russia. Popularity is just small begging for cult, we have plans for west because there's big potential for cult and worldwide in general.

APP: Everyone knows of founder Yegor Kresnov, what is the ethos that he has established with MKU and how did you come into leadership of the group?

MKU: Ethos of MKU is religion murder, me and Yegor are traditional satanists, we hold a lot of similarities in many ways. I found about cult in 2021, my outside activity started in 2019, by that time I was trying to get into dark aesthetics like siegeculture, etc and was making art had even few channels, after 2021 I started to talk to Yegor directly I wrote later Haters Handbook, year after published 2nd edition, I kept a contact with him by that time, last year I committed my first murder unknown to cult but only Yegor because of my safety, [redacted] I'm very proud I did it, I guess that's where my and Yegors trust became bigger and after old curator betrayed Yegor, he had no one closer but to put me as administrator.

APP: FSB has accused MKU of being SBU, SBU has said that FSB claims are only understood as a part of a "coordinated information operation which should only be viewed through the prism of hybrid warfare." Some people such as Italian sociologist Massimo Introvigne on the other hand claim that MKU is entirely fictitious and doesn't actually exist. For those interested in such conspiratorial views on MKU, what does MKU say to the public?

MKU: If we really worked with SBU our success would have accelerated much faster since someone would really help us with resources, after those rumors I even tried to get in touch with them, but they didn't cooperate with us, Feds shouldn't be trusted no matter it's SBU, FSB or CIA we work individually from anyone. First time me hearing on some Italian saying it's conspiracy which made me truly laugh now, only MKU carries over 50 kills and 150 other actions not talking on our subgroups, many achieved success including traitors just only because of us. Only thing I can say to public MKU isn't organization that is going to die that easy, everything just started and we gonna continue murdering on your streets.

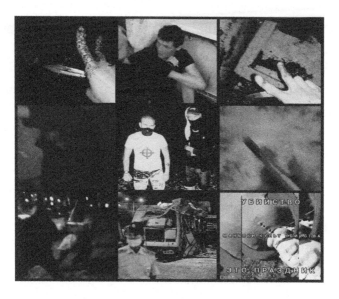

Montage of MKY photographic content provided to Drums of Tophet by Maniacs Murder Cult

APP: There is beginning to be public awareness of groups like 764 which have announced alignment with MKU though MKU has not been mentioned directly in news stories now circulating in the West.

MKU: MKU accepted its alliance with 764 only because of respect to 2 persons which was XOR and KUSH (leprosy), also XOR was man of action, I guess this alliance won't continue because there's no much potential of actions from 764 but we might still stay associates because they keep cleansing their own way by making weak suicide.

APP: Satanism and MKU - what are the primary dark spiritual currents at work within MKU?

MKU: Our main spiritual current that will always remain number one for us is Human Sacrifice. We have been associated with NSO9A and Satanic Front, both of them are offline at moment and NSO9A might not return. I find literature of O9A and Joy Of Satan most interesting personally but I don't like JoS at some parts where it comes that our religion isn't about evil.

APP: One of the most iconic images that circulate of MKU is the infamous photo with hockey mask - for those not reading Cyrillic are there any of these slogans you can share to public?

MKU: Most of our slogans are:

CLEANSING TO COME

MURDER IS CELEBRATION
WE WILL COME TO YOUR HOUSES AND MURDER EVERYONE

YOU WILL ALL DIE

Krumpfel

In blood-soaked field under somber sky stood sallow Krumpfel in ragged and tattered uniform, shirt tan and shorts black, flaxen hair combed sloppily to the side, Stygian jackboots perched upon a rubble pulpit.

Observing this little *führer*, the blue orbitals of enmity's children, sullen guards of fallen empire, their raging and perennial flames obscured by youthful veneers. Krumpfel spewed bitter daggers, utterances of apocalyptic immolation, *kleinen* holocausts of verbosity.

This once-unremarkable child, a pupil of mediocrity, in only half a decade metamorphosed into living icon of protest against *Die Kapitulation*, a roving terrorist of only fifteen years, youngest of his family, eldest in his court.

Brazen boys and girls of unbridled bloodthirst, their ribs leaping nigh out of their chests; a slenderness summoned by the ritual consumption of Pervitin, the patron deity of *blitzkrieg*, who manifested herself in the form of a pill. Their twisted ritual an unabashed mockery of Christian cannibalism – Goddess's body and blood.

With her guidance, this band of brutality made its way across Trizonesia, looting and pillaging, raping and killing, aided by sympathizers whose sweet informings allowed them to exact their revenge on those who had backstabbed their Fatherland yet again. This is all they knew, the stability of their youngest years as ephemeral as the society that raised them and now it had all come to an abrupt conclusion.

Before Krumpfel, the body of a traitor, one of their own who buckled under the immense pressure of finishing what *Der Führer* had started. Judas, as Krumpel now called him, led the occupiers to their den for a handful of sweets – the greatest betrayal. Dispatched as they were, more were soon to come. Sabotage had won the day, any chance of escaping fleeting.

Those angry eyes, those eyes who placed their lives and futures in the hands of their daring leader, fell unwaveringly on their monarch, their little prince. What worried him was not their defeat, it was their capture, for surely some great moral panic would arise at the notion of these 'misled' children being slaughtered, and although to be martyred would be desirable, it would force them to risk arrest for these same concerns occupied the minds of the enemy. Thus, they would abstain from slaughtering Krumpel's host. No good.

This is where the story ends – emulating their heroes to the bitter conclusion.

Pills passed around, from hand to hand, a capsule in every little palm. Pervitin′s patronage now substituted with that of Cyanide′s, the ritual all the same, and so it was their final supper, this millenarian cult, petite princedom, black horde. There would be no succession, no delivering of keys, the bread and wine, body and blood poisoned.

With all due reverence, there was no austerity of emotions. Smiles and laughs were exchanged, cackling as their bodies failed, leaving only the most beautiful of corpses, arranged to Krumpel′s aesthetic specifications. When all but he had passed, he delighted in the canvas he′d painted, an image of loyalty to the death, smiles stretched across their hardened yet tender faces. Then he found his spot, unbuckled his holster, and pressed his brother′s service pistol beneath his jaw.

Wurzburg

The clip of his hob-nailed boot upon the stone bridge monstrous, his thoughts, evil beyond all possible imagination except for his own. Wurzburg, a man of great appetites and foul - a man of great wickedness.

Beyond in the distance the snow-capped peaks of the Alps, beneath him the rushing accelerant white-foamed frothing river. Concourse of his soul, concourse to the cellars. White terror, cruel, catastrophic.

On the eastward shore he saw a team of horses struggling but healthily so with their burden, a black carriage. Plumes of steam from their nostrils, flesh straining against leather harnesses. As here, so below, down in the cellars.

Greta would be waiting for him soon, cold eyes peering out from one of the smoky beerhalls along the strasse - waiting for an appointed signal, a cryptic means of communication for a continued criminal undertaking.

--

Detention was a cruel thing, all the crueler when those who administered did so under the clear understanding that what was occurring was entirely illegal. When the potential uncovering of one's activities might consist of one's brains splattered across the wall from a gunshot in a similar cellar at best then the application of one's own lusts took small bridle. The attention came in matters of security, in matters of concealment, in preparation of the layers upon layers of deception necessary.

Wurzburg was knowledgeable in these matters, for he was an officer in the secret police of the new regime and all things in the land were not as they once had been. They had been injected with lightning. The sacrifice of death had given birth to all things new and fertile.

Greta had been his agent since time out of mind, for Wurzburg had decided that revolutionary excesses were surely to be had at the beginning of a revolution as surely as they were to be had at the end of a world war. Chaos had given him mechanisms to many things - Greta herself, a far weapon.

Down into the cellars they would go, amidst the screams, metal restraints all of the highest quality Krupp steel, metal chains, cuffs of all manner and both of them intricately wise as how to make their application the most excruciating. Angels of light theirs before an altar most obscene, wetted face, red blistered skin, sobbing, maniacal. Snarling, they would go about their business. "*Sodomize her!*"

Black-pigtails had Greta upon that infamous point of their first meeting - as Wurzburg climbed down from the coach on the eastern side of the fortress. Wagnerian chords of might blew through his mind as he alighted - the horses were testy but obedient, there was something in the air. Himmler-esque in her countenance, sharp featured, finest racial stock perfected far before a unified German state was a consideration. Child that had been born of cannon-fire and the strictest military discipline down through bloodlines stretching back.

A proper fraulein, potential already dark - the precision of classical symphonies ordered combined with the fell, foul sniff of the horrors that lie within the Alps - the horrors of the deep primeval forests, the darkness, the oppression. Together they would oppress.

Her brother had made the introduction, a high-riser in the regime - analytical, financier, entirely Swiss. His interests in the matter were somewhat inscrutable but he knew Wurzburg as a man of tastes, and to where such tastes lie.

Chaste enough, a professional relationship. She had contacts, circles into which certain influence could be enacted - access to certain elements that could be exploited under the social situation as it was now and increasing disharmony which would only accelerate.

She was a psychologist by trade at the time, though her pursuits were mostly academic - few clients - her family had money from ancestral acquisition, she was more interested in pursuing mathematics but political intrigue was everyone's game - Wurzburg more game than most.

Anything could have occurred at the family dinner at her father's estate - though predictably nothing did. The fowl was delicious, though all could have done with something more red, more rare. The conversation was well-behaved but perfunctory for the most part - Greta was a pernicious star of a foul constellation, she would have to be deployed. Her table-side flirtation was very subtle but recognized by him at least, by her sisters certainly so, by her brother least of all.

On the borders terrible things were afoot - terrible things engineered by him and his cohorts - the brother was not one to gloat, that sort of behavior not akin to his character, not akin to his breeding, but Wurzburg could tell that he was pleased. Their conversations had been in-depth in the halls of government - off-record of course, and he wasn't about to air his dirty laundry in the company of venerable parents and well-bred sisters. Still, you could tell that he appreciated having another contemporaneous colleague in the house and he appreciated the fact that introductions made on the inauguration of his own well-appointed and prosperous endeavors bode well for all.

Greta's sisters were all formidable in their own ways - but Greta was certainly the evil genius of the lot. Two of the older sisters were slated to be married soon - one of them to a notorious dragoon whose taste for horse-flesh, strong drink and dueling was renown - still political though, a man of property, conservative where it tended to count. The oldest sister, decidedly bookish, was betrothed to one of the mandarins at the intelligenciers - somewhat of a droll union from Wurzburg's perspective, but one that he could understand. The beloved baby of the family - quite rambunctious- still to early to tell.

Rolf bellowed at the end of the meal, a sign for everyone to make their departures - an amicable bellow. The baby sister chuckled, and rolled a fingerling potato off her plate. Greta's mother scowled, then laughed. Greta's father rose from the table, extending his well-wishes to Wurzburg before retiring.

Wurzburg stepped over a cat sleeping along the carpeted hallway of the home and made his exit from the house after pleasant good-byes. The sisters cast him a kind eye, though he knew he would be the subject of their talk and speculation later, Rolf he would be seeing again in several days time one office or another. Walking back across the threshold of the door he exited into the crisp night. Greta followed.

--

"What kind of wine do you prefer?" asked Wurzburg. Tawdry question, ill-thought out at least on the surface of things.

The sounds of the evergreens rustling in the winds suffused the atmosphere - air chill, healthily so, enlivening, even. She tipped her gaze upward slightly and a falcon flew overhead, wings and shape illuminated by the moon.

"That of my local country" said Greta, non-emotive, gaze looking now downward, procession of boots along the black dirt of the path leading further into the hills and beyond - the beginning of the forest proper.

"I like the wine that has been gained by conquest, the finer fruits sometimes accessible - sometimes not - by dint of trade, diplomacy and sometimes force of arms." Wurzburg responded, looking for a reaction, looking for a retort.

"Foreign wine is not so foreign if we look back through the annals of history" said Greta, a cold white hand snaking into his own, glint of similarly cold blue-grey eye reflecting lunar rays shining from above.

They walked long that night - longer than they each had predicted, longer than was wise for either in terms of responsibility, but shared destiny led them along, even so.

Up into the reaches of the hills where the dark shadows from the trees spoke of a spirit far more grounded, far more grave, than the most grim decisions made or might be made by the inhabitants down in the valley.

"I know what Rolf does along the borderland" she spoke, at one point, without prompting, once they were well into the forest, where things had grown darker.

"I ascertained as much" said Wurzburg, looking forward, acknowledging her statement only by verbal affirmation.

Above them the foliage of the forest began to churn - winds coming down from the Alps, primordial winds, uncaring of human involvement but not by initial apprehension malevolent - nor malevolent in truth by historicity. Greta and Wurzburg knew that however on this night they brought about something new - perhaps not new to their ancestors but at least new to them, new in the here and now. Within both of their mind's eye and in crystal visions they could see along those liminal spaces where the brother acted and where Wurzburg himself goaded - he the heavy man, he wielding the heavy whip. Piles of corpses exposed, naked and stark under the risen sun - uniforms similar to their own in some aspect, aligned ideologically in all truth, making good on a promise that long-written and foretold - from the scripts of the heretical monks to the pointed bayonets of the storm troops and then into the beyond. Amplified - accelerated - a dream made flesh. Their dream, our dream, all dreams.

"I would like to show you so much more than this Wurzburg" Greta whispered, the small sound of her voice almost indecipherable in the wind, the fact that Wurzburg apprehended it adding an emphasis that could not be denied.

She snaked her hand from his own, turning back - once only - white face, purest stock, flesh slightly reddened by exertion, then onward, onward, onward - toward the highest points of those small hills that lay in the shadows of the Alps, towards a destination mutual, exultant, triumphant. Foul and obscene.

Wurzburg licked his lips, hard to do, through thick mustache - taste of fowl and the day's consumption - he would go.

--

"What is this place?" Wurzburg screamed, astounded at what he had found, exacerbated by the exhaustion he felt in the course of the finding despite the fact that he was a young man, hearty and healthy in every respect in physicality.

Greta turned, turning her eyes entirely upward, toward fell and poisonous constellations above, toward the visions of stars crashing into stars, planets turning inward upon themselves and exploding - shattering filaments of their suicidal, astral destruction floating downward in crazed, spiral patterns.

"This, this, dear Wurzurg, is my grove!"

Greta laughed, peeling off her garments, nude except for her boots, then sitting down and removing them as well, flinging them some distance off, standing again and sinking her feet into the black mud that encompassed the area.

Wurzburg felt confused. Confused as to the situation, confused as to his guide and host and confused as to what was to come. She looked to him then, once again - steel-eyes, glinting in the moonlight. He felt himself transported and then, losing all sense of consciousness, normative at least, but still aware, he felt himself begin to arise. Beyond the rustling foliage of the Alpine forest, beyond the snow-capped vistas of the mountain peaks. Into stars, into time beyond time, into that which was beyond time, into the very ingredient of creation and destruction itself. There he floated, domiciled for a time and, in the grove, far below, Greta charted his course.

--

"Where am I!" Wurzburg screamed, the sounds of artillery deploying violent payloads surrounding him, the shouting of men suffuse around him - floorboards rumbling beneath his feet, walls shuddering under the influence of returning fire.

"Here, dear officer, here!" shouted one of his corporals, bound to him by office - loyal to him by emotion born from trauma shared in all ways, receiving and induced.

Wurzburg lept from the chair from which he had been sitting and scrambled under the desk - immediately upon doing so a missile penetrated the roof - infrastructure rained down, elements of the building imploding inward.

"To cover, to cover!" yelled Wurzburg to his men, those not already acting along such lines by their own recognizance.

He alone reached the trap-door, he alone to the basement - point of survival, point of life to continue his business of ending life. Succor for a time.

--

Greta appeared before him. Where had she gone? Where had she been? How did she come to him in such a place? Wurzburg began to stutter, astounded, afraid and Greta reached out a hand to soothe him.

"There, there..." she said, like a mother assuaging a babe at her breast. The mechanism worked, even as Wurzburg looked around him in a concrete cell filled with blood and human body parts - the carnal remains of his comrades, insomuch as they were, brief legacies smothered in bloody relief upon the walls of a fortress once his to control.

"It's alright!' Greta said, even though Wurzburg knew that all was decidedly not alright. How had this happened?

How had this catastrophe occurred, and to such a horrific degree, under his watch?

Greta blinked her eyes, full of care - wholehearted care in fact - but he could not understand. How had she come to him at this time? What was the situational measure of the operation? How had she come forth now? He did not know - and in increasing respect - did not care - her presence a balm to him, a healing potency. Ghastly, but healing.

She rose upon heels, picking up the body parts of his dead comrades - flinging them hither and thither - a look of resignation upon her face - yet her countenance one of love. Who was this child? If I could plumb the depths of this one then I would know, thought Wurzburg to himself, as his ears rung amongst the resounding cacophony of shells bursting upon his place of hiding - his very life inches away from termination, his death now more likely than life. Should I plumb the depths of this one, I will certainly know. his eyes fluttered and her cold gaze glared forth upon him. "Let me know, let me see!" Then to black.

As Wurzburg reoriented himself - how many hours past - Greta was gone, but the gore was still there. A junior officer shook him by the collar, demanding his consciousness to the present - whatever that present was. "*Achtung!*" the junior officer spat, and Wurzburg responded by spitting - in earnest - into the face of the one who had woke him from his revelries, whatever the situation. Even in climes of great peril, some semblance of order must be adhered to.

"What is the situation?" Wurzburg screamed, using the great-coat of the junior officer as a climbing mechanism to bring him foot by foot closer to standing position, then brooding above him - hands pressed upon his shoulders, driving the one who had awakened him downward.

"The allies, the allies!" the junior officer screamed, grasping the hem of Wurzburg's own uniform, shaking him. Wurzurg responded by smacking him across the face, no blood spilt in this internecine dispute, but head dully reddened all the same. He picked up his machine gun - ran to the door, already compromised - bursting it open with a kick of his boot - and began to fire.

Step by step was his procession amongst the muddy ground outside of the bunker. He saw his comrades-at-arms screaming, shot down man-to-man by blasting fire from a picking-off-point beyond his immediate vision but, by measurement, which he could ascertain. A boot to the shoulder sometimes - a boot to the face, quite often - he admonished them, flung them to reciprocal violence. He smacked a head against his own face, waking himself, and then smacked the face of another, pricking them to action - while his other arm deployed automatic-fire machined death to opponents occult to him, yet, by the sound of impact, obviously reaching their target.

He became the hero that day - Wurzburg, himself. The only one equal to the responsibilities of command - the only one branching out step by booted step, step by step upon bloodied and muddied ground to ground some semblance of order to what was hitherto as far as he could see a situation entirely chaotic. In such climes of chaos, anyone could win. He must make it his side, the very least he could do.

A soldier - one of the other side - gurgled what might have been his last breath - Wurzburg dropped his weapon, clanging against a shattered concrete piece of defense -

picked up the fallen banner of his foe, hitherto in the successful position up to that point, and shoved it into his opponent's throat.

Blood spurted upward in a prodigious spray, coating his face, his uniform, his stalhelm. Wurzburg laughed, then passed out, once again.

--

"Why can't I get there again, to that fabled supper, to that well-supplied table?" Wurzburg pewled, like a brat. Half of his right arm was bleeding out, covered in shrapnel, his breathing was arrhythmic, belabored. Through misty vision he saw other men around him - most of them in more dire straits than he himself - heads wrapped in second-hand gauze and even still pumping out the last rhythms of a life now in death, sacrificed in beatific melody to the limbic beat of the fatherland. Was he lucky? Was he simply a brat, a cad, eschewing all others to the hope that he could be the one to survive? He didn't know, didn't care really. A nurse appeared before him - soothing - hand upon temple, hand upon chest. Fuck this cow! he thought. His lips sneered. Greta or nothing, screw this cow-maiden - buckler to demographics that served no real purpose but acquiescence. He raised his hands dramatically, in a posture of some great violence but - then and there - he fell back into a stupor, wound-induced, bloody, unavoidable. All hell, he spat, as vision once again turned dark.

--

It was weeks until he came into himself properly again - most of the interim, liminal period at the hospital a fugue state which he in his most pointed consciousness could not readily ascertain nor remember. Even the apparent victory that he effected, that too was beyond him, having to be dileanated properly in the understood order by those who would weigh the situation politically as a win or a lose. The same nurse attended him, he remembered her. Now he found her quite pretty and felt remorse for his prior demeanor. She, being she, seemed to have taken no notice of his past behavior, though he could tell she appreciated his now more tempered demeanor and tender response.

'We won, Wurzburg, we one!" one of the head officers gurgled, between swills of Bavarian beer from a capped bottle, half of which dribbled down the jacket of the one who was amongst his appointed superiors. Wurzurg raised an eye and groaned, his body was wracked - his consciousness like an acrobat, akimbo.

Filament of the Book of Revelations smashed against his readings of philosophy - couldn't remember the authors - probably against party line, he wasn't in any situational place to care.

"You did it Wurzurg, you did it!" the senior officer declaimed. The spittle that issued forth from the officer's mouth created a visual spectacle that Wurzburg couldn't help but notice - flecks straining into the air, in the sun, maligned by dust, which streamed into the window above him. He was thinking too deeply, obviously, and the officer's enthusiasm wasn't commensurate to his own. very personal, brooding.

"What did we do, what did we do?" Wurzburg said at long last - he must speak, after all, he couldn't drive himself into a state of continual unprofessional posture, defeatism for the dogs.. The yield was what he expected, though moving forward, more than he could have hoped for.

"You dear Wurzburg, annihilated them!" - the officer almost spinning around in his revelry. Surely, with such a decidedly emotive reaction, the officer himself had some part to play himself? Wurzburg thought, though not really caring.

All of the forward positions of incursion - blasted to shit. Enemy personnel - killed or captured. Lines of engagement - now forwarded, by a great degree - by Wurzuburg's own incomparable heroism, according to the official report. Wurzburg was then happy, to a degree - now at peace - for the record. He reached upward for the senior officer's beer, taking it in his own hand with the shaky grasp of an old comrade, reciprocal more than generous, drink, and then again - on to the black.

--

"What's this nonsense, what's this abject stupidity!" Greta screeched, still attired in her nighttime garb, expensive white linen contoured salaciously to her small, lithe body, slightly more opaque than would usually have been via the dint of the profuse morning dew which coated both the landscape and herself.

Fritz, the hired hand from down in the village, scrambled at her command - attempting but not entirely successfully so to herd the mountain goats and render them into some sense of order for their morning grazing upon the hills that flanked Greta's father's estate. Greta would hear none of it, not in the mood nor disposition to resign herself to even the slightest disorder on this day of any days. She could still feel the filament of the star-dust upon her breast, denizens of an ancient, extraterrestrial race informing her own - superior, informing, commanding. Rolf had sent her a message that things had gone decidedly south amidst the conflagrations taking place on the northern front - though his own machinations along the borders were going, as ever, clockwork. Fuck the brother! she bellowed internally, amidst the agricultural tumult unfolding before her in the immediate. What of my lover?

Jenny ran as fast as her little legs could carry her - attempting, but failing, in reigning the livestock in line. Greta's brows arched insanely, malice in the very heart. She hated theses chores, she hated the expanse of beautiful countryside - she hated the reich, even. A few clients awaited her later that day - fractured minds to plumb, experimental methods to be employed in the curation of the same. She had her correspondents in Switzerland who provided guidance - she had her reading, her erudition, her own theories to employ as well. But here she was, relegated to disgusting chores in early hours - skewing her mind, waylaying her genius. Fritz was a simple peasant - if he erred - he ought to be shot, she thought to herself. Jenny, the little sister - hers - not his - ought be thrashed within an inch of her life for subpar performance - but the father, both their fathers, ought to be tortured to the point of death for the abject political exploitation of making either of them toil in such a manner amidst the atmosphere of such pastoral bliss, even though they owned it - because they owned it. Greta was disgusted. She'd thrash Jenny to death as an existential experiment - she could imagine it - the screams, the blood, the audial admonishments leading to fright, then terror, then horror, then full panic - but it wasn't wise in the short-term, not wise perhaps in the long-term. Father would be mad, especially at a killing blow. Jenny was only more than half her age, slightly - her junior a dawdling, toddling dummy comparatively - she building a firm psychological practice and still only entering into what life had to offer. Perhaps some mercy, perhaps.

Set upon a clime, clime upon a clime, clime upon a precipice - pushing them over. Greta mulled her patients thus, thinking great thoughts - thoughts that would set actions in play - some disastrous, few benign, all pointed. Her own thoughts of the morning foray into the green fields of her familial estate weighed upon her to a degree - she subliminated, tried to do so, aware of the fact - but they still played back. Such annoyed her, obnoxious. Murder was not an option - especially not for such cosmetic misdeeds - yet she still entertained the width and breadth of such a scenario, and in great detail. Why did she do this to herself? Why to be amped up on such dread fantasies? She could still, possibly, give her little sister a prodigious whipping - that would be the most genteel and potentially accepted outcomes - some release for her, herself, some horror wrought amidst the family - for Jenny herself, specifically, though Greta didn't really care about her one way, or the other.

Greta had already pushed forth certain formulaeo in the span of a working day - ergo, a few hours at most - that would send those already with heads spinning, already suicidal, into further trauma - self-induced trauma, but really, trauma induced by her - building upon the building blocks that was the foundation. She didn't think herself cruel, professionally - though she knew she was, psychologically, carnally, certainly so. These were small excesses that couldn't really be quantified - wouldn't be quantified. Recorded, yes, but as a matter of record in the most perfunctory of ways. Greta was safe to slay mightily in her way, for the time, according to her assessment.

Fritz she would glady kill, she thought to herself. Kill in a perfunctory manner, with little thought - and no thought afterward, having to think of him no more the treat, the delight in absence. But he was useful, in his small but fundamental way. Greta hated having to think of such nothing persons, such chattel. Jenny on the other hand she could whip, whip to the point of potential death - but not beyond. Humiliate in the course of doing so to such a degree that her brain would be scarred irrevocably - forever. Should she be a client of Greta then in the thereafter? Greta would charge her in Swiss francs - or whatever the most modern, stable currency was at the time - whatever took her fancy and would bring some fiscal advantage. She mustn′t make it easy for her, little sister, she must make it hard - she should engineer the trauma - then cure the trauma - attempt to cure the trauma - while exacting the ultimate price. Little brat. She'd had thrashed her to all hell and ruination here, now, if the situation had been more linear. Perhaps she had whipped her sister to a degree most severe and then, in turn, her father would have whipped her. His violence however would have not matched her own, rather a paltry experience, for them both. Greta could spare him that, at very least. No need for subpar undertakings that close to death. In his thirties, certainly, an event to be had - relished - exulted in, however shamefully so - one ought not to spank then fuck their own daughter, but in current circumstances it would simply be sad. That depressed her, depressed Greta mightily, she walked away then and there from that pastoral scene - no use to continue - what occurred there would occur, if her oversight wasn't to par, so be it. Husbandry wasn't her profession, a rural hand and a directionless similar daughter of her line - not really her responsibility.

The walk to the sanatorium had been a grand one, although ghosts of the morning came to haunt her albeit briefly latterly in the afternoon. She had dressed meticulously. Black dress, dark stockings, sturdy, shiny black witch-like shoes polished to a high gloss. Hair attired in ringlets in the Teutonic fashion descending down from the hills like astral death come down from the heavens - all who passed by her in well-apportioned carriages greeted her with due deference as was her station. The clean air of her Alpine home filled her nostrils and she felt for the first time that day a sensation of freedom - a clear assessment of the arena for experience and wide possibility that lay before her. Future association with Wurzburg would be yet one more keyed mechanism in that tapestry. Great things awaited her - fell and terrible, sweet and tender, each unto their own season.

--

Hydrotherapy was a brutal cure, at least in the way it was applied in the institution in which Greta was employed. Surely not the hydropathy as she proscribed it for herself - dainty body in waters just hot and steaming enough, curing ails of the mind and body admist flower scents amplifying the purity, pale and auric glow of a most delightful, special and erudite young fraulein of the reich. Even things that are nice can become torture if they are applied unwillingly, and even those natural aspects that in general enhance life can lead to catastrophe when taken to the extreme - as the gentle wind upon still waters become a hurricane, as the gurgling, life-giving mountain stream become as torrent of flood, as the sun glinting upon white snow, bringing bloom to hearty winter flower transforms to lethal avalanche.

"Apply additional liter volumes" Greta spoke dispassionately to her assistants, a man and a woman, both large, possibly married. Both in white coats, the man bald with great prodigious mustache - the woman of ample girth but exceedingly strong, her hair attired in ringlets like Greta's own, such was the fashion, though her own hair was blonde turning quickly to grey and the style was somewhat obscured by the nurse's cap perched upon her head. The woman secured the patient in the bath by the shoulders, to prevent whatever struggling would yet occur despite the fact that the patient was bound by straight-jacket, bound tightly and soaked through - the man hefted a great metal cistern braced against his thick chest and began to pour, water and ice sluicing down upon the patient's head.

The patient's lips pulled back in a horrified rictus - skin bluish, unnaturally white - the tell-tale signs of not simply coming age but a coming apart of mind and psyche. This was good, this was what Greta wanted to see. A neurotic from Basel, her neurosis had become dangerous - lunging out with a carving knife at her husband while seated around the family table. Greta could understand, hypothetically, the impetus for the woman's crimes however such actions almost certainly brought about a fate as that which the lady found herself in now - or worse.

From the open windows high upon the walls of the chamber Greta could hear the bells of the cathedral ringing in the one o'clock hour - she pulled her own watch from a small pocket and checked for syncopation - all in order. She waved at the nurses and they withdrew the patient from the bath - wriggling and cursing like some cruelly set upon eel. They stripped her of her straitjacket at which point she immediately tried to lash out violently - the matron smacked her across the face, her cheek lit up an angry red, and the patient thought better of it. Stripped of her robe, also soaked. Coldness, nakedness. Greta looked at her, eyes belying little disguised disgust. Up then upon a metal gurney, hoisted like meat, naked flesh against cold stainless steel, medical grade. Strapped down with leather straps and wheeled away to some other part of the hospital.

Greta looked around her - the entire atmosphere of the chamber magnified a certain sort of horror - the sort of place where intestines might be spilled upon the floor with the machined whirring of an electric mechanism from some future nightmare and then washed away, perfunctorily, before moving on to the next pastime, also grisly in nature. The acrid scent of disinfectant filled her nostrils and she rubbed a hand against the front of her coat, slightly damp from the condensation of the room, slightest pressure against burgeoning breast beneath. She gazed into the sunlight beyond the window, obscured by strange clouds that began to turn there. Something unnatural in the firmament this day, a feeling of others' wars, beyond any mortal conflict that she or her kith and kin could even hope to engineer. When would the sickle drop? Soon.

--

Several days later Greta's rage erupted against Jenny and no mercy was spared her. Similar circumstances - morning chores gone awry, by no fault of her own, Greta thought to herself, even though she was the one appointed as to the responsible oversight for their completion without undue complication.

The air had grown more chill that day even though the sun shone mightily upon the snowy mountaintops, causing the river to rush more fiercely as ice melted far above, large drifts, many very great in size, melting and falling into the churning waters.

Greta's afternoon schedule would include mostly letter writing, inter alia, at her small study up near the attic, but no trips to the clinic, no clients as such, so the interim hours were therefore hers to do so as she pleased.

As Jenny fumbled in her given tasks of mid-morning Greta allowed her own frustration to seethe within her, inward only, outwardly nothing - spoken rectification done so with mild reproach only - she allowed her own ire to build, malice, lust for punishment, to a cataclysmic degree - redirected though, pleasure in pain to be waylayed. But when it was to come, at what volume. This thought gave Greta great hope.

After all had been done as needed to be done they walked along together for a time, the course Greta's suggestion but with Jenny's most enthusiastic and girlish acquiescence. Silly child, damnable child. Needful of punishment - perhaps needful and deserving of much more. Down to the gorge, down to see where the concourse of the accelerated water turned brutal to true.

Greta walked ahead of her on some of their journey down, setting the pace, charting the course. She smiled and delighted inwardly as she could hear her little sister struggling with no small degree of trouble in attempting to keep up with her, the more limber, long-legged, older sister. One-step equaling several of her junior partner. Greta espied from the corner of her eye and appreciated the discomfiture she caused, the added trouble - really not necessary, but an added enhancement nonetheless. Had Greta herself been taking this path even in a most hale and hearty of moods she would have had been at least several degrees more relaxed, but she enjoyed adding that extra something - Jenny suffering much more than her herself, more suffering to come, according to plan.

As they edged closer Greta allowed Jenny to take the lead, they could both hear the sounds of the river now, almost cacophonous in report - soon they would be showered with the cold mists spraying upward, dancing upward off the rocks. This area was littered with stones of generous size that had to be traversed or avoided by sometimes laborious detour. To Greta's amusement and to Jenny's credit the little sister more often than not chose the former, Greta watching her legs pump vigorously upward upon the craggy surfaces before then disappearing on the other side, foot to German skirted hem, then head obscured only to appear once more, negotiating yet another obstacle.

"Crown of creation" muttered Greta to herself, feeling within the pocket of her coat for a straight-razor which wasn't there but for a moment, then finding it again, the heft giving her comfort, the potential for lethality.

Greta the watcher as sister moved point by point closer to destination - always within sight. It would be next to nothing for Greta to move in closer herself should she so choose, at a moment's decision, closing the gap.

One of the last trees presented itself to her then and there, birch devoid of leaves, the color of corpse, color of death. Greta maneuvered her way up the trunk, delighting sensually in the way the hardness ground against her - withdrawing straight-razor surgically, opening it against the bark, watching how its shining steel reflected the light - cutting a sturdy branch, sturdy enough, but supple, for her purpose, sliding down again.

She caught her little sister, just as the outcropping shown itself upon her line of vision, as the wind became almost gale force, as the spray anointed them both. Jenny pleaded, screamed, as Greta raised her skirts and then rained down blow upon vicious blow upon legs that kicked, seeking to escape. Greta's eyes raised appreciably as red lines formed upon skin whitest upon white, then the blood began to drip.

When Greta thought that little sister had suffered enough, least that she had caused enough suffering that she could get away with, Greta let the defeated body drop, ignominiously. She pivoted away, ever so briefly, one foot, to gather white mountain flowers upon her hand, then blotting the wound - spreading red upon white flower petals - then turning, flinging them into the churning waters of the rivers beneath her, watching them waft downward to be consumed - her memorial, her sacrifice. In black meditative state she drifted her gaze once more - little legs punished now raised, militantly pumping once again, fleeing her sadism. Over the edge of the rocks went Jenny, limbs pumping against nothing but the wind and spray now, she fell - disappearing into the foam, sucked under by the waters.

--

Cathedral bells began to ring later that day - Greta had stood long looking into the waters, too long, her shock immobilized her and it was nigh half and hour before she was able to move at all, and then to begin to coverup, to attempt to evade.

Alarm was in the air before she made it back to the borders of her estate, for the river flowed down to the direction of the town and a man had spotted the twisted child body washed up against a berth - the authorities quickly summoned - the signs of fresh beating noted - and, being of a prominent family in an area close-knit, the corpse almost immediately identified.

Greta trembled almost uncontrollably as she walked across the expanse of green toward the entrance to her home - Fritz was tending the goats on the high fields by this hour, Rolf still on his near travels, and her other sisters hated the outdoors. The tolling of the bells however were still a cacophony even at this distance and those of her kin domiciled inside would soon burst forth, like birds roused from the bushes by the hound in the concourse of a hunt.

As she negotiated which entrance to take - there were three for her choosing, as well as outbuildings in which to hide, for a time, the nauseating sound of a motorcycle roaring up the drive assailed her ears. Greta turned and looked, instinctively, though perhaps by doing so compromising her instinct to survive intact. Greasy, black leather trenchcoat, jack boots, goggles. Cap bearing insignia, ruddy face. She began to run - she was recognized. Wurzburg.

She burst through the door of the house, all sense of cover blown to pieces, her father saw her from an adjoining room and started to raise from his chair unsteadily - the chittering of two sisters in the direction of the kitchen went suddenly quiet.

Up the stairs, her limbs pumping more furiously than Jenny's ever had, for she was more limber, more athletic - she was alive.

She heard the shouting begin even as she ascended the second flight and by the time she reached the door of her study the shouting had become a small roar, growing closer, interspersed with the sound of pursuit - they were after her now.

Greta entered the study and slammed the door behind her, slamming the bolt shut with equal measure - fastening it securely, though in these circumstances the security it offered was negligible. She flung her clothes off, dressed again in garb more uniform, more mean. Hair pulled hastily out of the braided ringlets that reminded her of her little sister, her society - pulled out with too much strength, strings of hair ripping out and positioned betwixt her fingers. Now she was the nasty witch she was meant to be, she laughed to herself. Wild, unbound hair evidentiary of such a state. Now the constellation of her life had turned to total ruination and catastrophe - moreso to come however if she did not end it while she had a chance.

Greta searched the top of her desk for anything edged - scissors, letter-opener - she doubted if either of those would be sharp enough to do the job which she intended with any modicum of accuracy and efficiency - though grisly such an application would surely be. In her panic she managed to swipe the majority of the contents of the wooden surface upon the floor, books thudding askew, papers floating chaotically, an antique inkwell shattering. The pounding had begun at the door now, as if every member of the household was doing so at once, amidst shouts which spanned from dire pleading to harsh and threatening recrimination. Greta screamed in response, picking up her desk chair and hurling it against the door, hurling it with such force that it burst into its individual components despite a decidedly sturdy make. She knelt down and grabbed a blackened shard of the broken inkwell and began to carve a jagged concourse across her collarbone and neck, growling as she did so, perspiration dripping down against the ink creating horrible, spider-web like rivulets against flesh.

Black-ink mixed with sweat, sweat mixed with blood, though her acumen at suicide ultimately proved quite paltry, less than terminal. Still, the blood mixed with black provided grisly aesthetic - grisly enough, at least, not near as grisly as the true death of her sister.

The banging came on the door in a more extreme measure now and it was no longer the fists of her parents and surviving sisters but the boot of Wurzburg - sole produced for war, body wielding ramped up on Pervitin - in time the latches burst forth, her concealment compromised, and the horde poured forth.

"Gudrun, please!" cried Greta, her eldest sister the first to spring upon her, slapping her face repeatedly, grabbing her shoulders and shaking them before commencing to slam the body of her sister repeatedly onto the floor. Greta felt the pain but felt oddly alive, the situation like a dream, but a dream in which she was gaining sustenance, however foul in nature. Gudrun was pulled off by multiple hands, familial and otherwise. Greta could hear her mother muttering in a wheezing voice, "*polizei, polizei!*". Others, screeching in multiple iterations of the same question, what had she done to Jenny? What indeed had she done, and why?

Wurzburg curled his fingers into her unbound hair and lifted her to standing position - the pain felt good - Greta felt maniacal, she began to laugh, hysterically, in earnest insanity. Family cursed her, spat, hands and fists lunging out to harm her, to register their protest against her decidedly criminal action - they felt puerile, weak, ineffective. Wurzburg swatted them away even as he proceeded in dragging her by the hair, out from the door of the study, across the threshold, down the stairs. Greta took the event sensually, howling with each expectancy of offense and ignominy - simply a black theatre. Wurzburg and her the only actors. She perhaps the only actor. Gudrun, mother, father and the rest only set and setting - if that.

Through the front door - the van of the *polizei* proper waiting for her then, Wurzburg's motorcycle thrown to the ground in haste. Three men stood against the back of the vehicle, gated door thrown open in expectancy, criss-crossed iron bars waiting for new, choice entrapment - a now pale sun still causing the officers' rubberized leather jackets to gleam sickly. What would they do, what could they do - all options open, moreso sadistic, moreso grim.

Tears stung Greta's eyes - everything was falling apart, her median now torn asunder, normalcy as it was upended - life in acceleration.

Wurzburg wrenched her into standing position - by the hair - brutally so - then flung her into the arms of his comrades, liers in wait.

Irons were clapped upon her, only after hands drawn back violently behind her.

She hissed, she spat, but she also wept - protest at this stage only being aesthetic, futile in any real way beyond that of appearance.

Greta could tell some of the men reveled in their professional capacity - whereas at least one of them was horrified at the extent of the crime they felt she was guilty of, which might prompt that number to be even more excessive in application of justice, and discipline, once their wits were about them.

The sounds of her family faded in the background - she wondered if father would die of shock, she wondered if Gudrun might plot her murder. Probably glad to be rid of her in anycase, Gudrun, her and Jenny, maybe. The latter simply an embellishment to family life which Gudrun would soon leave by dint of marriage, Greta a potential embarrassment - strange, unsound. Gudrun need not do anything now, did not have to do anything - the wheels had been enacted by Greta, Greta to bear the brunt, Gudrun only having to act in such a fashion to preserve her own station.

The officers dragged her into the back of the van, bashing her small frame against the sides of the doors as they did so - she screamed - one of them rared back a leather-gloved fist and smashed into her stomach, scream stifled. She panted. He sneered. Shoved in rudely, she could feel one of the men's gloved hands grope her between the legs and on her rump as so doing - this undoubtedly only the beginning of such ministrations and at as an of yet tender age, despite her profession. These were not the old days however, the days in which a landed family despite tragedy might see one such as she herself carted off to a convent on the far side of the Reich. These were the days of revolution and in days of revolution punishment was applied vigorously, profoundly, for by so doing one showed elan - and by such elan lay survival, even prosperity. Her kin were wont to prosper, and so they shall even in dark circumstances. The sorrow they felt today would soon pass, her other sisters and her brother would sooner than nought breed their own little Germans which her parents could bandy upon their knees, to pat their heads and listen to their idiotic coos. The shame of Greta's alleged atrocity would last longer than the sorrow of the loss of Jenny's life, but that too and in the present environment would fade. In grim contradistinction, Greta's journey into the dark had only just begun.

She sat herself upon the hard metal bench inside the van, huddled against the back, three Gestapo there with her. Her restraints were further secured, leg iron around one ankle quickly detached, ran through a ring in the floorboard then reattached. A leather strap apparatus was brought down across her upper waist then likewise secured to mechanisms attached to the walls of the vehicle. These, sickly familiar to Greta herself, for she used variations of the same in the context of her work at her institute - what she would give to be intramural there, now, within.

They began to move and through the secure grates at the back of the van Greta could watch the curious scene of her childhood home slowly disappearing - growing smaller and smaller until it ceased to exist. Her mother, fallen to her knees, surrounded by her sisters - Gudrun's cries sorrow mixed with rage, her mother's simply defeat, despair. Her father at the door of the house, gripping his chest. Would he survive the ordeal of his daughter's malfeasance? These figures - nearest and dearest - or at least, for her, the most familiar, began to disappear themselves along with the hills, the valleys, the yonder Alps. She saw Wurzburg mount his conveyance and grow close to the rear of the van - for a moment so close that she fancied she could even see a blotch of red upon face cold and pale - before he whipped around the side and overtook them. Would he be waiting their upon their arrival on the *strasse*, would he be waiting for her down in the cellars? She thought he would.

Only a matter of twenty minutes from her erstwhile estate did Greta know that she wasn't headed to the station in the town, two hours out from that Greta realized that she wasn't being renditioned to the larger station in the capital of her state. Where were her captors taking her? The sun began to set over the horizon - large, orange, scintillating along the edges - color far too rich in hue. Disgusting, nauseating.

One of the guards, the one who had secured her further for the ride, chose the lengthening dark to rub his hand against her thigh - he could have done so without any recriminative action before sunset, but perhaps the night put him in the mood. Gauging no real reaction worth noting from Greta he ceased altogether after very brief attention. No harm, no foul. The other guard, closer to the window, had steadily taken draws from a metal flask secreted within his jacket and now began to nod off slightly. Earlier while taking his tipple he had stared out blankly. Something troubled his heart, Greta though to herself. Separation from a lover far away, or even the ubiquitous existential crisis. *Acta deos numquam mortalia fallunt.*

Wurzburg watched the night as did Greta, he already at what would be, for a time, a shared destination. He had gone ahead then aside, a ride alone to an unmarked airfield - through three checkpoints, inside the wire, then onto a very highspeed conveyance that covered several hundred miles in minutes. Such was his ranking, such his priority of mission.

Her journey would not be as comfortable, albeit also by air. Trundled into a cargo area of a larger plane, military carrier, still shackled, definitely blindfolded. Still in flight however, and that said alot. Would that they both be naked, rubbed from head to foot in the fat of the slaughtered - would that they both cross a black sky, chill of the Harz upon their flesh. Would that they both be lashed amidst the howls of the wilderness, both proferring the profane kiss to beastly Satan - would that he were her true sister bound in hideous unity. Times to come.

Wurzburg's regular domicile had been anything but regular - but the closest to home that he could auger would have been at the desk adjunct to the cellars - the realm of black cabinets, the origin point of multiple conspiracies conceived by him, enacted by his fellow compatriots and then executed in deception upon his victims. And, once renditioned to the place of their punishment, the place of his cohorts discipline thus so enacted - how they would be punished, to the very limits of discipline, severe straining the limits of the imagination.

He found himself now at the outer regions - in the periphery - his cruelty had drawn him thus, not by his own ambition but by the observance and surveillance of his superiors as to his acumen for the profound, the monstrous. By their assignment destiny splayed forth like an organ ripped apart. Wurzburg stood at the railing of a watchtower in one of the many camps - camps of unthinkable horror - and, as an insider, far more foul in truth than what historicity would deign to tell.

The anti-aircraft lights cast the entirety of the thousand acre compound in a dread luminous light. One-thousand points of light. He considered the statement to himself, drawing a pull from a metal flask - brother to the metal flask that the secret police guard accompanying Greta had imbibed, frequently, with relish. Wurzburg had so provided, for if the man was sober he would have raped her tender flesh. Wurzburg knew his men, they knew him only insofar as he disclosed - deception, all.

Wurzburg missed the black cabinets, the subterranean lair from which his adult persona and professional career had been largely forged - the garbled screams echoing down the corridors, the surety of the iron gates clanging shut in their obscene authority - the myriad safes filled with currency by which he procured myriad services, their procurement secret, no record except in the resultant repression which sliced through the land like a diseased wound designed to fester. He himself ran most of the left revolutionary groups in his sector - left revolutionary in name, high reaction in truth, according to the accepted terminology. One safe for the funds dispersed - another for the receipts should blackmail be needed, which was seldom if ever, though best to hedge one's bets, so thought Wurzburg. Time enough for the cellars in future, they would still be waiting - high reaction thought some, high revolution thought he, white revolution.

Wurzburg gazed across the camp and for a moment the natural light of the half-moon - nominal in its luminescence amidst the artificial shadow planet glare - was obscured, coinciding with the cacophonous engines of the bulldozers and other working machinery which populated the punitive zone in vast profusion. Faint semblance of a smile passed his lips as he saw a pile of naked human corpses pushed into a tetrahedral shape, moon thus so obscured, before falling as the bodies fell, rolling into the vast pits that had been partially constructed by the recently deceased themselves. he rubbed his hands against his chest, his stomach, the front of his trousers. He felt female. What that he was a vulture to alight in the brutal cascade of the dawn and thus so feast.

In the far distance he could hear the screeching of an airfleet in flight - then the bass reverberations of the bombers dumping their payload onto cities and villages already paralyzed by fear. They were the hawks, much more hawkish than their counterparts amongst their national adversaries, for the operators in the reich in which he operated were bound in ideology - not ideological in the fashion that the simple would auger it but ideological in the true sense in that they would do so and had done so continually, stretching back into the mists of prehistory - though they knew not why.

What was the purpose of the twin-headed eagles of empire facing imperiously outward if not to feast upon those on the periphery and then beyond? What was the purpose of the wings of the eagle if not to outstretch - to take to the skies - assessing, analyzing, dominating, possessing? Surveillance led to power - Wurzburg knew this - as did the layman, in theory, but their theory was weak. Only by the doing was the science - a black science at that - known in true. Wurzburg had done alot - but he must do much more.

Greta lay on her belly in the cargo hold of the military transport plane - her vision obscured by blindfold not of thoughtless scraps of motley but by an expertly sewn apparatus designed for just such a specific usage. She appreciated this detail though she knew that her vision would be mostly nominal any and at all as the cargo hold was dark and the secret police representatives there present were ensconced even further into the shadow than she. She felt the cold of the metal surface of the floor against her cheek - her face turned to the side, depressed, face likely facing the interior wall as she could imagine that the point of her nose was close to some similar surface but more meandering in shape.

Rather than to succumb to the dread of what might come which she knew in her heart of hearts was an infinitely futile pursuit - animal at least in the human animal conception, she chose instead to engage in fantasy more appropriate to her station and profession, strictly in the sense of Lacan, though that in itself might be hubris on her part. Only the droll would engage in self-critical introspection in such circumstances however, Greta thought, and her crime seemed to her - the one real on-the-ground observer - as more the hand of God than an act selfish and base - though she might have been the catalyzing factor.

Greta imagined Jenny spinning upon a spinning wheel - too large and complicated a contraption for her young state - for in the fantasy Greta so envisaged her younger sister was, at least in this phase, concrete only at the age of her death. Surrounded by tall wooden walls fashioned by expert craftsmen of an age gone by, she was secure. Jenny was neither attired in the vague garments of a fairy-tale age, nor wearing a more traditional garb of era current to her death - that, somewhat antiquated in truth, though still prevalent, and still more very much revived in the *volkisch* revolution of their once shared present. Little sister was nude, the humiliation suited Greta, she reveled in it, the more it was a discomfiture to Jenny, the more the revelry was increased for Greta.

See there the curve of Jenny's little posterior upon the sturdy chair, wrought of similar workmanship and wood as the walls which imprisoned her? Greta could see the lesions of red criss-crossing the hips so exposed - some of the wounds, still bleeding. Was Jenny a saint? In certitude not - simply a silly little child who had been soundly punished and scolded as children were often. But the severity, the expertise - the fact that the harm still bore out - that must denote that Jenny was not simply naughty but bad, profoundly bad. That evidentiary state pleased Greta greatly. Bad child, naughty child - child that perhaps should not be. Jenny labored greatly at the spinning wheel - so clumsy, so inept. Neither the infant who in its inherent stupidity would be doted after nor the succulent youth of great promise, as was Greta herself - and certainly not the girl fully matured, a woman really, whose swelling flesh and licentious hormonal demands seemed choice societally but which remained philosophically puerile. Just a thing, just a nuisance. Neither here nor there. Spewed forth if judiciousness held sway, contained in great anxiety among normal sorts.

Greta stationed herself behind one of those great beams comprising the wall of the enclosure - a small hole drilled just for such purposes of her surveillance. She allowed herself to be girlish in this fantasy, she giggled at her little sister's discomfiture. She tugged at one of her black braids and then another, ringing her head like a bell - she flittered her eyes, she stuck out her tongue - her mocking, clandestine. Full-force girlishness now hers to have, full-force horror to be employed by her own hands, should she wish it. Was this child before her still living, or was it dead? Was it beholden to her still - older sister - not the oldest, but the most noxious, by reputation at least - even in this state? Did she inhabit some in-between borderland in which Greta could still prick her as she chose? Pleasure in great profusion in that option - a torment, perhaps, eternal.

Made in the USA
Monee, IL
02 May 2025